To Patrick and Brendan,
Happy Reading!! ☺
Elissa Grodin

N is for Nutmeg

A Connecticut Alphabet

Written by Elissa D. Grodin and Illustrated by Maureen K. Brookfield

Text Copyright © 2003 Elissa D. Grodin
Illustration Copyright © 2003 Maureen K. Brookfield

Sleeping Bear Press
310 North Main Street, Suite 300
Chelsea, MI 48118
www.sleepingbearpress.com

Sleeping Bear Press is an imprint of The Gale Group, Inc.,
a division of Thomson Learning, Inc.

Printed and bound in Canada.

10 9 8 7 6 5 4 3 2 1

Library of Congress Cataloging-in-Publication Data

Grodin, Elissa, 1954-
N is for nutmeg : a Connecticut alphabet / by Elissa Grodin ;
illustrated by Maureen K. Brookfield.
p. cm.
Summary: An alphabet book that introduces Connecticut's history,
culture, and landscape, from the state bird, American Robin, to the
letter z in Noah Webster's dictionary.
ISBN 1-58536-124-0
1. Connecticut—Juvenile literature. 2. English
language—Alphabet—Juvenile literature. [1. Connecticut.
2. Alphabet.]
I. Brookfield, Maureen, ill. II. Title.
F94.3 .G76 2003
974.6—dc21   2003010469

To my parents.

ELISSA

⚓

In memory of my mother who rekindled my love for painting.

*Thanks to Heather Hughes and Sleeping Bear Press for the opportunity
to grow creatively and explore new horizons. And to Barb and Jennifer…
thank you…it's a pleasure to work with you both!*

MAUREEN

A is for American Robin,
a lovely little fellow.
He sings a pretty tune,
musical and mellow.

During the 1940s there was a movement to adopt a state bird. Hearings were held at the state capital on the subject. Three requirements were established at these hearings for the qualities our state bird should have: 1. that it is frequently seen, especially by children, 2. that it have beautiful plumage, and 3. that it have a beautiful and easily recognizable song. The American Robin fit the bill perfectly and was adopted as the official state bird in 1943.

Robins' eggs are so beautiful that a special color was named after them, 'robin's egg blue.' Artists like to paint their nests so they can incorporate this wonderful color. Next time you go to a museum, look for one in a still-life painting.

A a

Bb

B is for Mister Barnum,
and his animals and clowns.
He started a traveling circus
for kids in all the towns.

Phineas T. Barnum was born in 1810. Although we remember him as a circus promoter of Barnum & Bailey fame, during his lifetime Phineas was a leading citizen in his hometown of Bridgeport. As mayor he did many good things, such as creating city parks and bringing industry to Bridgeport's economy so more people could have jobs.

His first sensation as a showman came when he was only twenty-five years old. Phineas featured Joice Heth, a woman claiming to be 161 years old and a former nurse for George Washington. (She was eighty.) Phineas had a success putting Joice on exhibit for people to see. Later in Barnum's career, Queen Victoria of England became furious when he bought Jumbo the Elephant from the London Zoo. Jumbo became the circus's star attraction.

In 1831 Prudence Crandall, a young Quaker woman in her twenties, was invited to head a girls' school in Canterbury. She accepted, and the school was very successful.

When Sarah Harris, an African-American girl, applied, Miss Crandall admitted her, but the local citizens did not want Sarah there. They vandalized the school at night, throwing rocks and smashing windows. Angered at their bigotry, Miss Crandall decided to change school policy and made it for black girls only. Enraged, the townspeople were able to get a law passed that forced the school to close. Miss Crandall appealed the case in court and won, but vigilante violence forced the school to close for good. She moved out west in 1835 and continued her work as an educator. In 1886, near the end of her life, Miss Crandall was awarded a pension of $400 a year, as an apology from the state of Connecticut.

Because of her great courage, Prudence Crandall is Connecticut's state heroine.

C is for Miss Crandall.
When everyone said 'no!',
she opened up a school
for those who could not go.

D d

In 1966 a man named Edward McCarthy was operating a bulldozer, clearing land for a building site. He discovered something so amazing that it put a stop to the building ever getting built. He had stumbled upon hundreds of well-preserved dinosaur footprints from hundreds of millions of years ago, left during the Jurassic Period. Tracks from all sorts of dinosaurs are preserved at Dinosaur State Park in Rocky Hill. In fact, the Connecticut Valley has the most dinosaur tracks and footprints in the whole world.

A large, three-toed track of *Eubrontes giganteus*, our state fossil, can be seen at Dinosaur State Park. Thousands of Eubrontes tracks were found in a single layer of rock.

D is for Dinosaur State Park—
There are fossils all around,
and hundreds of dinosaur footprints
are buried in the ground.

E is for Explorers
who left their homes behind,
and sailed across great oceans
to see what they would find.

Captain Adrian Block set out from Holland and sailed across the Atlantic Ocean with a fleet of four ships, *The Little Fox*, *The Nightingale*, *The Tiger*, and *The Fortune*. In 1613 the fleet arrived in New Amsterdam, now known as New York, and anchored there. While in the harbor, *The Tiger* caught fire and burned completely. Capt. Block built another ship, *The Restless*, which he sailed across Long Island Sound to Connecticut, leaving the rest of the fleet behind.

The wooded shoreline of our state looked invitingly green and lush. Capt. Block found the mouth of the Connecticut River and sailed up to explore. There he encountered Native American tribes. Eventually Capt. Block established a trading post, where Hartford is now. He traded tools and other goods with the Native Americans for furs, which were an extremely profitable item with the Europeans back home.

Our state was one of the original 13 colonies established by European settlers. In 1639 a new government was created by using a set of laws based on a democratic philosophy, saying that government should get its power from "the free consent of the people." These laws were called the Fundamental Orders, and they were based on the writings of Reverend Thomas Hooker, a scholar and clergyman. They represent the first outline for a democratic government. Later, Thomas Jefferson would use these same ideas to construct the Declaration of Independence.

The state flag was adopted in 1897. Its motto, *Qui Transtulit Sustinet* is Latin for "He who transplanted still sustains." It refers to the transplanted Europeans who thrived in their new land.

F f

F is for the Flag,
blowing in the breeze.
Made of silk, in blue and white—
A sight that's sure to please.

G is for a town called Groton
where the first nuclear submarine
was built to go underwater,
so it would not be seen.

Did you know that there is a submarine capital of the world? Groton is home to *The USS Nautilus*, Connecticut's official state ship, which was the world's first nuclear-powered submarine. Atomic (nuclear-powered) submarines can stay underwater for almost unlimited amounts of time. They have actually gone around the entire globe without surfacing.

The building of *The USS Nautilus* was finished in 1954. Eventually, submarines became capable of firing missiles. Once that happened, their role during wartime changed from sinking enemy ships to firing at land targets inside enemy borders.

G g

H is for Hartford,
the capital of our state.
Inside the gold-leafed dome
is where we legislate.

You can see Hartford's magnificent gold-plated capitol dome for miles around, across the Connecticut River lowlands.

Reverend Thomas Hooker left his home in England in search of greater religious freedom. He first settled in Boston but was unhappy with the leadership there. He had heard of a fertile valley along the Connecticut River, so he decided to establish a settlement there, with a small group of his parishioners. They named their settlement Hartford. Around 1636 Hooker united Hartford and two other settlements, Wethersfield and Windsor, creating the Connecticut Colony. In 1638, based on Reverend Hooker's writings, the very first written constitution was drawn up, as a foundation for local government. That is why one of Connecticut's nicknames is "The Constitution State."

Charles Ives (1874-1954) is our state composer. An 1898 Yale graduate, insurance executive, and Pulitzer Prize winner, Mr. Ives was a fascinating man, full of paradoxes. He considered himself to be an old-fashioned Yankee, and used traditional Yankee hymns in his compositions, especially in his famous Fourth Symphony. Yet his music is considered ultramodern. He was so original and unique that a word was coined to describe him and his music: *Ivesian*. This adjective means, "to be yourself."

Each year on the Fourth of July there is a fireworks celebration at the Charles Ives Center in Danbury.

I i

Charles Ives

I is for Charles Ives,
who wrote symphonies and songs.
Alongside great composers
is the group where he belongs.

If you wanted to be a lawyer in the early 1700s you would have to find a lawyer who was willing to teach you. There were no law schools yet.

In 1774 Aaron Burr asked his brother-in-law, Judge Tapping Reeve, to tutor him in the law. Judge Reeve decided to teach a few other students along with Aaron, and when there got to be too many students to fit in his parlor, he built a one-room schoolhouse behind his home in Litchfield. Soon he had 50 students in what became known as the Litchfield Law School. In this and other early law schools American law, as distinct from English common law, developed.

Aaron Burr went on to become vice president of the United States. Other graduates included Supreme Court Justices Ward Hunt, Levi Woodbury, and Henry Baldwin, as well as Noah Webster and John C. Calhoun, another future vice president.

J is for Judge Reeve
who started something new—
A school made for lawyers,
room enough for just a few.

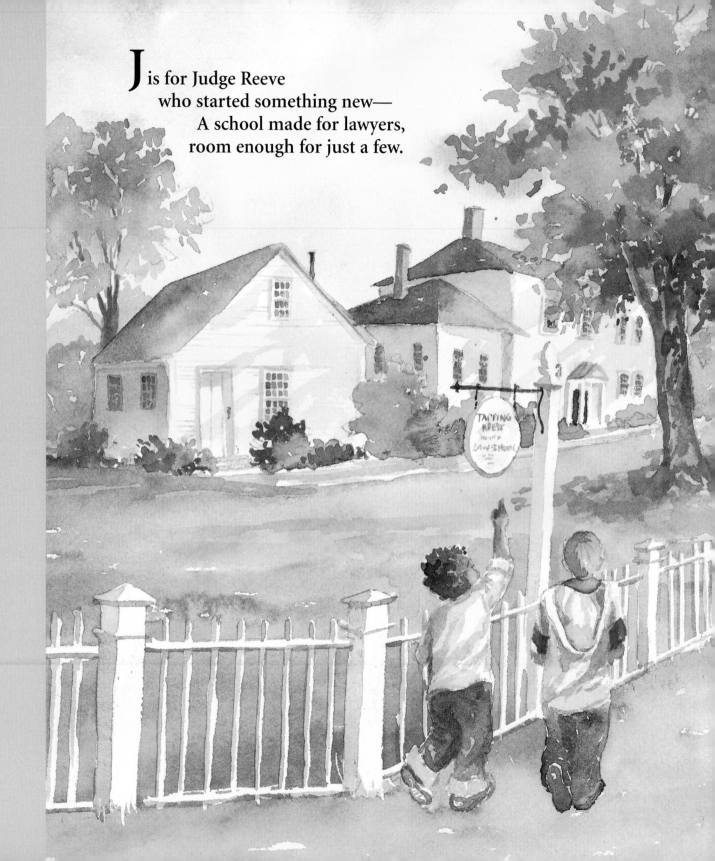

K k

As one of the original 13 colonies, Connecticut was settled by people from England who wished for more economic and religious freedom than they had back home.

Our state hero, appropriately, lived during that exciting time of fighting for freedom. Nathan Hale was a schoolteacher who, during the war of independence, joined the fight. Nathan was in an elite group of soldiers known as Knowlton's Rangers. When General George Washington asked for a volunteer to sneak behind enemy lines in order to get important information, Nathan volunteered. He was captured by the English on his way back, and hanged as a spy, at the age of twenty-one. He is best remembered for saying, "I regret that I have but one life to give for my country," but his personal motto was, "Waste not a moment."

K is for Knowlton's Rangers—
They wanted to be free.
This special group of soldiers
fought with bravery.

Most people know what an architect does, but what about a landscape architect? Frederick Law Olmstead (1822-1903) was born in Hartford. While traveling in England, he took a great interest in the beautifully designed landscapes there, especially admiring the work of eighteenth century designer Capability Brown. When a plan for Central Park in New York City was proposed, Olmstead and his English colleague, Calvert Vaux, submitted the design that was chosen.

This great landscape architect designed some other famous places, such as the grounds of our nation's capital, the park system in Boston (called "The Emerald Necklace"), the Chicago World's Fair in 1893, and many more.

Ll

L is for Landscape architect,
designing beautiful spaces,
city parks a mile long,
and other important places.

FREDERICK L. OLMSTEAD

M is for Mountain Laurel,
    with blossoms of pink and white.
Also called the calico bush,
    it makes a pretty sight.

M
m

Although it's really a shrub, the mountain laurel was named the state flower in 1907. Its beautiful pink and white flowers, made especially vivid and bright by the background of dark green leaves, have attracted the attention of travelers since colonial times. It was first mentioned in John Smith's "General History" in 1624.

Commonly found, the mountain laurel is also sometimes called Calico Bush and Spoonwood.

Our nickname, "The Nutmeg State," embodies the idea of resourcefulness. The early days of our state were characterized by inventiveness and know-how, qualities described by the term 'Yankee ingenuity.'

Yankee peddlers were traveling salesmen who went from town to town and colony to colony with a horse and cart or wagon. These mobile department stores sold an astonishing variety of goods—just about anything you could think of: furniture, tools, clocks, books, mirrors, pots and pans, fabric, sewing notions, and spices, to name a few.

Nutmeg was a popular spice, but very hard to get since it only grew in the far-away tropics. Occasionally a peddler was known to carve one out of wood and sell it as the real thing, which is how we got our nickname.

n
N

N is for the Nutmeg State
  but please don't be misled—
These aren't exactly real ones
  but carved from wood, instead.

O is for Eastern Oysters
      caught in Long Island Sound.
Along with all the lobsters,
      they're the best fish to be found.

The Native Americans and early European settlers ate huge quantities of oysters, which thrived naturally in the tidal rivers and bays of our state. Farmers began cultivating oysters in Long Island Sound, and by the end of the nineteenth century led the world in the oyster industry, shipping oysters all around the world.

Oyster shells are planted in shallow water that is not too salty. Baby oysters then fasten themselves to the shells and grow. The oyster is our state shellfish because oyster farming has always been a thriving industry and was an important part of our early economy. Connecticut oysters are sold all over the United States, and several of Connecticut's cities host annual oyster festivals.

P is for Praying Mantis,
a fascinating creature.
He blends among the leaves
with green as his main feature.

P p

When a bill was proposed to the state legislature in 1977 to adopt a state insect, school children were allowed to speak at the hearings. They nominated the praying mantis because it is so beneficial to farmers by eating crop-destroying insects. Some kids said they make good pets, too!

Praying mantises appear in our state from summertime until the weather turns cold. They are harmless to humans, and eat things like flies, grasshoppers, moths, and caterpillars. They get their name from the way they appear to sit quietly, holding their two front legs together as if they were hands clasped together in prayer.

Quinnehtukqut is a seventeenth century Native American word meaning, "beside the long, tidal river." This was a reference to our state's longest river, the Connecticut, and it is the origin of our state name.

Hundreds of Algonquin-speaking woodland tribes lived all around the state, thousands of years before European explorers and settlers arrived. They fished and farmed along the state's many rivers, the three largest being the Connecticut, Housatonic, and Thames. If you lived at that time, you would certainly want to live near a river, for several important reasons: the river was an abundant food source, the riverbanks were fertile land for growing crops, and the river was a primary mode of transportation.

Q is for Quinnehtukqut,
a Native American name.
When you say Con-nect-i-cut,
it really sounds the same.

In 1796 a plucky and independent young woman named Amelia Simmons wrote the first American cookbook. Published in Hartford, the complete title was *American Cookery or the Art of Dressing Viands, Fish, Poultry, and Vegetables and the Best Modes of Making Pastes, Puffs, Pies, Tarts, Pudding, Custards, and Preserves, and All Kinds of Cakes, From the Imperial Plumb to Plain Cake, Adapted to This Country and All Grades of Life.* Quite a book title!

American Cookery contained mostly recipes from English cookbooks, adapted for the first time for Americans. This splendid little book stirred great feelings of patriotism when our country was so young. It was a sellout. *American Cookery* has been reprinted and is available to us today. Here is a recipe from it:

Indian Slapjack
One quart of milk, one pint of Indian meal, four eggs, four spoons of flour, little salt, beat together, baked on griddle, or fry in a dry pan, or baked in a pan which has been rub'd with suet, lard or butter.

R is for old Recipes
collected in a book,
which people liked to read
so they could learn to cook.

The sperm whale was designated our state animal in 1975 to honor the contribution it made to the early economy of our state. In the 1800s the whaling industry was the main reason for New England's booming economy.

Thousands of people worked in the whaling business. Owners became wealthy from it. Sperm whales were the most popular kind to hunt, even though they are very aggressive, and have been known to sink a rowboat full of whalers. Sperm whales are now considered an endangered species and may no longer be hunted.

Other types of industry have replaced whaling over the years. With relatively few natural resources, manufacturing supplies the most jobs in our state. There are a few thousand farms left, and commercial fishing still makes up a small part of our economy, as well.

S is for the Sperm Whale,
   this animal is gigantic.
He makes himself at home
   swimming the Atlantic.

Ss

From William Shakespeare to Jane Austen to Mark Twain, one thing all great writers have in common is that they are successful students of human nature, with a deep understanding of all the things it means to be human.

Samuel Langhorne Clemens was such a writer. As a young man he worked as a Mississippi River boat pilot. This is where the pen name, Mark Twain, under which he wrote comes from. 'Mark twain' is the river call for water two fathoms deep, meaning safe passage for a riverboat. He settled in Hartford with his wife Olivia, and that is where he wrote his novels *Huck Finn* and *Tom Sawyer*.

In his works Mark Twain helped us see the problems of the world and at the same time, be able to laugh and stay optimistic.

T t

T is for Twain, a writer—
    One of the best there's ever been.
He wrote about Tom Sawyer
    and a boy he called Huck Finn.

U is for *Uncle Tom's Cabin*.
It was written here, you know:
A very important novel
by Harriet Beecher Stowe.

HARRIET B. STOWE

An important novel, *Uncle Tom's Cabin* was written by Harriet Beecher Stowe and published in 1852. The title character is a faithful slave whose owner falls into debt and must sell him. Another slave, who is to be sold along with Tom, decides to run away and find her husband, who escaped on the Underground Railroad, a secret network of people who helped slaves escape to freedom in the north. Tom decides not to accompany her and continues on in his life of slavery and pacifism.

Born in Litchfield, Harriet Beecher Stowe (1811-1896) spoke out about ideas that were unpopular at the time, such as outlawing slavery and getting women the right to vote. She helped to change the course of history by writing this book, which convinced scores of people that slavery was cruel and wrong, and contributed to the eventual abolition of slavery.

In Hartford, Stowe's home has been restored as a museum and is located across the lawn from the Twain House.

Uu

V is for Mystic Village
where over a hundred years ago
fishermen hunted whales
with harpoons and nets in tow.

JD DRIGGS
SHIPSMITH

Mystic is a fascinating recreation of a nineteenth century shipping village. At that time, nearly every family in town was involved in the boat-building business. You can still visit the shops along cobblestone streets where sails and crows' nests and every other part of the ship were made and sold. Mystic has been in the boat business since the 1600s, building any kind of vessel you could think of: whaling ships, clipper ships, pirate ships, and during World War II, navy ships.

Before it became illegal in 1856, during wartime citizens were allowed to use their own boats to help by harassing enemy merchants at sea. They were called privateers, and when a war ended, some would become pirates. During the Revolutionary War, privateers were buzzing all over the Mystic River, helping protect Mystic Village by attacking any English vessels they could find.

W is for Eli Whitney—
As a boy he loved to tinker.
The things that he invented,
prove that he was quite a thinker.

Eli Whitney (1765-1825) invented the cotton gin (short for "engine"), a machine that allowed farmers to harvest cotton much faster, but his real legacy is assembly-line production. He devised the mass-production system in factories, where previously goods had been made one at a time. He was a key player during the Industrial Revolution, when our country was changing from a farming society where people used simple tools into a more modern society of factory-manufactured machine-made products.

True to the reputation of 'Yankee ingenuity,' our state has had a wealth of inventors. The first patent ever issued to a woman was in 1809 to Mary Kies; the method she devised of weaving straw with silk thread was a boost to the ladies hat industry. The lollipop and Pez candy were invented in a New Haven candy factory. When employees at William Frisbee's pie factory threw a pie pan around at lunchtime, the Frisbee was invented.

You don't think of mystery and intrigue when you think of a tree, but our official state tree has plenty.

In 1662 King Charles II of England gave the people of Connecticut a charter, an official document allowing the right to own land. In 1687 when King James II tried to get it back, there was trouble. He sent soldiers to retrieve the charter and take away the rights that went along with it. At a famous meeting around a large round table between the king's men and representatives of our state, the candlelit room suddenly went dark. Legend says that Captain Joseph Wadsworth plucked the charter off the table and stashed it outside in a big oak tree. The charter was safe and it was never returned to England. The white oak was named our state tree in 1947 in honor of this exciting adventure.

X

X marks the spot
inside an old oak tree
where something once was hidden,
as part of a mystery.

Y is for Yankee Doodle,
a dandy of a song.
Silly words and a catchy tune
make it fun to sing along.

Y y

Although we can never be certain of the author of this familiar children's song, it is said to have been composed in 1755 by Dr. Shuckburgh, an English army surgeon. He watched as a group of colonial soldiers passed by. They were so poorly dressed that each man had stuck a chicken feather in his cap to create a more uniform look. The song is actually meant to mock their shabby appearance. 'Macaroni' was a slang term of the day for a sharp dresser, or a dandy. The word 'Yankee' originally came from the Dutch word *Janke*, which means 'Johnny.' (Dutch sailors used it to make fun of English settlers.) Eventually, it became a nickname for New Englanders.

"Yankee Doodle Dandy" was voted our official state song by the state legislature in 1978.

Before there were dictionaries, people spelled and pronounced words however they wanted. Noah Webster (1758-1843) devoted himself to writing dictionary-type books so that everyone in America would agree on spellings and pronunciations.

Born in West Hartford, Mr. Webster attended Yale, became a lawyer, and eventually a judge. He had a lifelong interest in all aspects of language: the formation of words, how language changes over time, and word definitions. This interest led him to write his first book, *Elementary Spelling Book*. It was wildly successful and sold a million copies a year. Pioneer families used it to teach their children to read out on the frontier. Schools used it as a textbook and settlements used it to hold lively spelling bees. Mr. Webster continued writing dictionary-type books. *An American Dictionary of the English Language* was published in 1826.

There is a special word for people who compile dictionaries: lexicographers.

Z is for the final letter
in Mr. Webster's book.
He found a meaning for every word—
Imagine how long it took!

A Quinnehtukqut Quiz

1. Why is Prudence Crandall the state heroine?

2. Our state bird's eggs are so beautiful, they even had a color named after them. Can you name our state bird?

3. What is *Uncle Tom's Cabin* and what impact did it have?

4. Noah Webster was a lexicographer. What does this word mean?

5. What is the state tree and why?

6. What Connecticut resident invented the cotton gin?

7. Who designed Central Park and where is it located?

8. What is special about Groton, Connecticut?

9. Where did the name of our state originate?

10. Our state hero is famous for saying "I regret that I have but one life to give for my country." What is his name?

Answers

1. This Quaker woman fought to give African-American girls an education when it wasn't allowed.

2. The American Robin is our state bird.

3. This powerful novel convinced a lot of people that slavery was wrong and helped work to abolish it.

4. A lexicographer is someone who compiles dictionaries.

5. The white oak was named our state tree because of the famous Charter Oak that supposedly hid a document from British soldiers.

6. Eli Whitney

7. Frederick Law Olmstead designed Central Park in New York City.

8. Groton is where the very first nuclear-powered submarine was built.

9. It came from the Algonquin word *Quinnehtukqut*, meaning "beside the long, tidal river."

10. Nathan Hale

Elissa D. Grodin

Elissa D. Grodin grew up in a large family in Kansas City, Missouri, and was fifteen years old when she started to write short stories. While living in London in the late '70s, she wrote for the *Times Literary Supplement* and *New Statesman*. After moving to New York, she studied at the School of Visual Arts and met her husband, actor Charles Grodin, while interviewing him for *American Film* magazine. Elissa lives with her family in Wilton, Connecticut. *N is for Nutmeg* is her first children's book.

Maureen K. Brookfield

Artist Maureen K. Brookfield lived and studied in the New York/New Jersey area for many years. She has attended the Parsons School of Design, the Art Center of Northern New Jersey, and has studied with several nationally known artists. Her work has been widely exhibited and is represented in numerous private collections. Although she has worked in many mediums, watercolor has become her favorite means of artistic expression. Now residing in Marshfield, Massachusetts, Maureen is active in local and regional art associations. She is the illustrator of *E is for Empire: A New York State Alphabet*, also published by Sleeping Bear Press.